W9-DJG-350

To our beloved husbands, Tim and Brian.

With love and affection and
visions of many private romantic moments,

Lisa and Mona

Love 'N' Romance

Lisa Tawn Bergren

ILLUSTRATIONS BY

Mona Weir-Daly

MULTNOMAH BOOKS - SISTERS, OREGON

LOVE 'N' ROMANCE
published by Multnomah Books
a part of the Questar publishing family

©1994 by Lisa Tawn Bergren and Mona Weir-Daly

International Standard Book Number: 0-88070-711-9

All illustrations by Mona Weir-Daly

Edited by Shari MacDonald / Designed by David Uttley

Printed in Hong Kong

Most Scripture quotations are from The Message ,©1993 by Eugene Peterson.
Also quoted: The New International Version ©1973, 1984 by International Bible Society
used by permission of Zondervan Publishing House.

For information:
Questar Publishers, Inc.
Post Office Box 1720, Sisters, Oregon 97759

93 94 95 96 97 98 99 00 01 — 10 9 8 7 6 5 4 3 2 1

Author's Note

The longer I'm married, the more I understand the importance of the basic building blocks of loving relationships. Although most of us know these elements and understand them well, I think all couples should be reminded over and over what is at the foundation of this thing called "love." I've teamed up with my childhood friend Mona, now a professional illustrator, to bring these ideas alive. May this book be a delight to read and an inspiration for many fun and romantic moments.

Lisa Tawn Bergren

Friendship

FRIEND, n. one attached to another
by affection or esteem.

"My spouse is my best friend!"
My parents said this over and over, affirming to
me, to each other, and to the world how important
Dad was to Mom, and she to him.
Examine your friendship with your partner,
and set out to enjoy life together: exploring, learning,
seeking, dialoguing, and understanding.

FRIENDSHIP

[Love] burns like a blazing fire,
like a mighty flame.
Many waters cannot quench love;
rivers cannot wash
it away.

SONG OF SONGS 8:7 (NIV)

Love must cease to be
a supplement to the real and become
reality itself, which it always was.
Like a low lovely hum, you must sense
it always in the background.
Like the soft ringing of bells in the wind,
you must feel the sound.
Like a heartbeat of the mind, you
must always know it is there.

HUGH & GAYLE PRATHER
NOTES TO EACH OTHER

10 Romantic Notions:

1.
Call a local radio station and dedicate a song to your love.

2.
Trace your family roots way back. (Tim's married to royalty!)

3.
Set a weekly "date night" that can only be interrupted by a severe emergency.

4.
Trek through the Himalayas together.

5.
Place flowers in every room of the house.

6.
Enter any sweepstakes that promises a trip for two.

7.
Sing in a choir or join
another church group together.

8.
Watch your wedding video together.

9.
Set a table—complete with linen and china—
in the middle of a field or on a beach (someplace
isolated), and have your meal catered.

10.
Take a safari on the African plains.

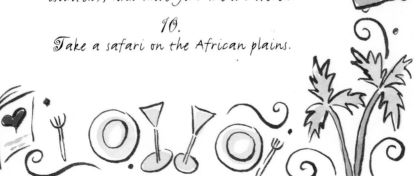

Kindness

KIND, adj., having the will to do good
and to bring happiness to others.

How different life could be
for so many couples if they concentrated
on being as kind to one another as
they are to others!
"Be kind" is an age-old bit of advice that
goes a long way in relationships of love.
Never say things to your spouse that you
wouldn't say to other friends.

SPECIAL ROMANTIC NOTIONS

Doze in a
hammock together on a hot
afternoon or on
a cool summer night, under
starry skies.

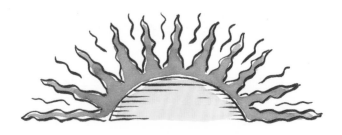

10 Romantic Places to Visit:

It might take fifty years, but I'm bound and determined to see all these places with my husband. Choose a few locations you'd like to visit with your own spouse, or make your own list. Happy traveling!

1. A Swiss chalet (so cozy...)

2. A rustic, old Farmhouse (hearken back to simpler times...)

3. A deserted Tropical beach (you are all alone...)

4. The ruins of a European castle (he's your dashing prince, and you don't look so bad yourself...)

5. A quiet stream in a shady Forest (peaceful, private...)

6. A turn-of-the-century Grand hotel (try Many Glacier Lodge in Glacier Park—extremely classy...)

7. A cruise on the Nile (does it get more exotic than this?)

8. A gondola in Venice (a romantic must— there's no getting around it...)

9. A cozy (intimate) B&B on the coast of Maine

10. A street-side café in Paris (hot coffee, long looks...oo-la-la!)

Passion

PASSION, n. an ardent affection;
love; deeply stirring.

I am bowled over by the gift
that God has given me in my husband.
When I allow myself the luxury
to really think of all he is to me,
I feel a deep, abiding,
all-encompassing passion for him.
Christ loves His church with a passion;
try and capture that same depth of
love for your spouse.

*Let's not just talk about love;
let's practice real love.*

1 JOHN 3
(FROM THE MESSAGE)

Love is the Great Transformer...
Love transforms:
Ambition into aspiration,
Greed into gratitude,
Selfishness into service,
Getting into giving,
Demands into dedication,
Lonliness into happiness.

UNKNOWN

SPECIAL ROMANTIC NOTIONS

Buy
two wonderful rocking chairs
in which you'll "grow old"
together.

Companionship

COMPANION, n. one much in the
company of another.

Who is in your company the most?
If it is anyone other than your partner,
check your priorities.
God has given you a mate with whom you
are to live and love. Spending time
together builds shared memories,
shared experiences, shared feelings and,
consequently, a stronger marriage.

Tenderness emerges
from the fact that two persons, longing,
as all individuals do, to overcome the
separateness and isolation to which
we are all heir because we are individuals,
can participate in a relationship that,
for the moment, is not of two
isolated selves but a union.

ROLLO MAY

SPECIAL ROMANTIC NOTIONS

Narrate
a video that details the history of
your love; use old pictures, letters,
and intimate memories.
Hold a private showing on a
special occasion.

Affection

AFFECTIONATE, adj. feeling or showing a great liking for a person or thing.

Studies show that babies crave human touch;
without it, they do not develop normally.
Do we lose this desire as adults?
Certainly not.
Most people need the reassurance given
through hand-holding, a back rub, a tender
touch on the cheek, or a steady, loving gaze.
Don't hold back!

*Post this at all the intersections,
dear friends: Lead with your ears,
follow up with your tongue,
and let anger straggle along
in the rear.*

JAMES 1
(FROM THE MESSAGE)

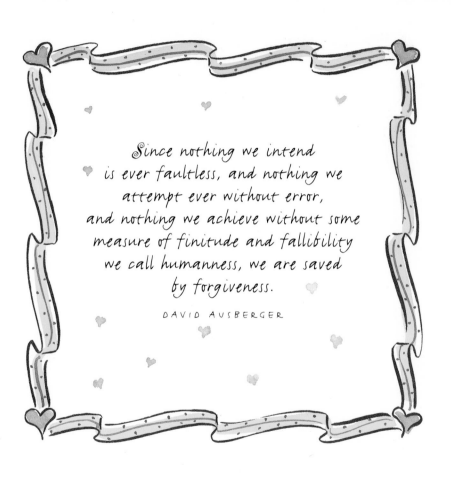

Since nothing we intend
is ever faultless, and nothing we
attempt ever without error,
and nothing we achieve without some
measure of finitude and fallibility
we call humanness, we are saved
by forgiveness.

DAVID AUSBERGER

14 Romantic Songs:

1. "True Companion"
(COHN), RECORDED BY MARC COHN

2. "When I Fall in Love"
(YOUNG & HEYMAN), RECORDED BY CELINE DION AND CLIVE GRIFFEN,
NAT "KING" COLE, JOHNNY MATHIS

3. "Unforgettable"
(GORDON), RECORDED BY NAT "KING" COLE, NATALIE COLE

4. "I Will Always Love You"
(PARTON), RECORDED BY WHITNEY HOUSTON,
DOLLY PARTON, LINDA RONSTADT

5. "An Affair to Remember"
(WARREN, ADAMSON & McCAREY), RECORDED BY VIC DAMONE

6. "Something Good"
(RODGERS & HAMMERSTEIN), RECORDED BY JULIE ANDREWS AND
CHRISTOPHER PLUMMER/SOUNDTRACK FROM THE SOUND OF MUSIC

7. "Somewhere"
(BERNSTEIN & SONDHEIM), RECORDED BY NATALIE WOOD AND
RICHARD BEYMER/SOUNDTRACK FROM WEST SIDE STORY

8. "A Kiss to Build a Dream On"
(KALMER, RUBY & HAMMERSTEIN II), RECORDED BY LOUIS ARMSTRONG

9. "You Bring Me Joy"
(LASLEY), RECORDED BY ANITA BAKER

10. "Have I Told You Lately"
(MORRISON), RECORDED BY VAN MORRISON

11. "Say Once More"
(GRANT & COLE), RECORDED BY AMY GRANT

12. "Always On My Mind"
(THOMPSON, CHRISTOPHER & JAMES), RECORDED BY WILLIE NELSON

13. "I Will Be Here"
(CHAPMAN), RECORDED BY STEVEN CURTIS CHAPMAN

14. "The Way You Look Tonight"
(KERN & FIELDS), RECORDED BY FRED ASTAIRE, FRANK SINATRA, BILLIE HOLIDAY

Forgiveness

FORGIVE, v. to cease to feel resentment
against; pardon.

Oh, the walls that resentment builds!
As God forgives our repented sins,
casting them "as far as the east is from
the west" and "into the deepest ocean,"
strive to do the same with your
love's mistakes.
Then get up, brush yourself off,
and move forward.

We are each of
us angels with only one wing.
And we can only fly embracing
each other.

LUCIANO DE CRESCENZO

SPECIAL ROMANTIC NOTIONS

Take out
an ad in your local newspaper
(a full page or a few lines
in the personals) publicly
declaring your love.

Intimacy

INTIMATE, adj. of a very personal
or private nature.

Rejoice in the mate God has given you.
Celebrate your partnership by
sharing intimate dreams, desires,
and doubts. This is the person with whom
you should form deep connections.
Sharing promotes intimacy.

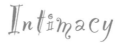

SPECIAL ROMANTIC NOTIONS

Travel
from one end to the other
on the Orient
Express.

"THE WORLD BELONGS TO THOSE WHO HAVE SEEN IT." — ANONYMOUS

1. Spend a quiet evening at home. (Send the kids to a friend's home for the night.)   2. Write love notes and insert them throughout the book your partner is reading.

10 Ideas for Intimate Moments

(Be sure to figure out ahead of time how you'll get back.)

3. Walk along the beach together,
one in front of the other. Be careful to follow the
leader's steps as exactly as possible. Feel the
contours molded in the sand by your partner's feet.

4. Take horseback riding lessons together.
Explore paths that go deep into mountain forests,
or along quiet beaches.

5. Pray together. If you're uncomfortable
praying aloud, do so silently at the same time
after agreeing on several things
you both want to pray about.

6. Hold hands.

7. Tell each other what you thought
the first time you met: how you noticed that his
smile reached his eyes, how your
heart pounded, etc.

8. Float down a stream on inner tubes. Pause at a riverbank for lunch.

9. Give each other back rubs with bath oil; foot rubs with peppermint lotion.

10. Begin each morning with a lingering, tender hug.

Communication

COMMUNICATION, n. message; an exchange of information.

When you talk, try stretching beyond the usual, "How was your day?" Be more direct. "What was the best thing that happened to you today?" "How are your colleagues treating you?" On a deeper level: "Where do you think we are in our relationship on a scale of one to ten?" and "Why?" The healthiest married couples I've seen are those who work to build excellent communication skills.

Trust steadily in God,
hope unswervingly, love extravagantly.
And the best of the three is love.

1 CORINTHIANS 13
(FROM THE MESSAGE)

Commitment

COMMIT, v. to give in trust.

He's yours and you're his
through thick and thin (including
waistlines), the good times and the bad
(even if you can't balance your checkbook),
for better, for worse (for keeps!).
Knowing this instills an enormous sense of
security. Daily promise yourself and your
spouse to always make them
Number One.

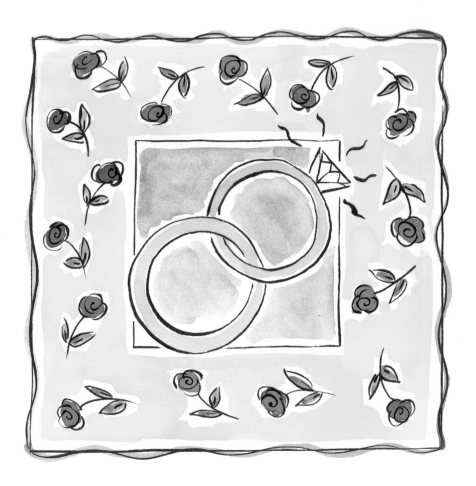

SPECIAL ROMANTIC NOTIONS

Invest
in a surprise balloon ride
for two at sunset or sunrise.
(A guide should
come, too.)

19 Romantic Movies:

1. Beauty and the Beast
2. The African Queen
3. The Princess Bride
4. Far and Away
5. The Sound of Music
6. The Man From Snowy River
7. Return to Snowy River
8. Gone With the Wind
9. Random Harvest

Honesty

HONESTY, n. fairness and straightforwardness
of conduct; integrity.

You know when you're not telling
your mate the whole story.
Every time you hold back or change the
facts, even "a little," you jeopardize your
relationship. Without trust, your
relationship will crumble. Tell the truth,
the whole truth, and nothing but the
truth, no matter how painful
it might be.

When in doubt, tell the truth. - Mark Twain

Love never gives up.
Love cares more for others than for self.

Love doesn't want what it doesn't have.
Love doesn't strut, Doesn't have a swelled head,
Doesn't force itself on others, Isn't always "me first,"
Doesn't fly off the handle,
Doesn't keep score of the sins of others,
Doesn't revel when others grovel,
Takes pleasure in the flowering of truth,
Puts up with anything, Trusts God always,
Always looks for the best, Never looks back,
But keeps going to the end.

1 CORINTHIANS 13
(FROM THE MESSAGE)

The measure
of one's devotion is doing,
not merely saying.
Love is demonstration, not
merely declaration.

ANONYMOUS

Appreciation

APPRECIATE, v. to recognize with
gratitude; expression.

Tim and I have fallen into the easy habit
of casually thanking each other for the small
(and big) tasks each of us performs.
A "thanks for taking out the garbage,"
immediately neutralizes the resentment that
can arise when a jointly shared chore is done by
one. Suddenly, the act is seen as a gift of
love. Appreciation goes a long way
and takes little effort.

ALSO BY

LISA TAWN
BERGREN

Romantic Notions

ROMANCE NOVELS:

Refuge
Torchlight
Treasure